Ascribe to the LORD the glory due His name. Bring an offering
and come before Him; worship the LORD in the splendor of His holiness.

~ 1 Chronicles 16:29

Shout for joy to the LORD, burst into jubilant song with music.

~ Psalm 98:4

He will yet fill your mouth with laughter and your lips with shouts of joy.

~ Job 8:21

O Lord, our Lord, how majestic is Your name in all the earth!

~ Psalm 8:9

The LORD will watch over your coming and going both now and forevermore.

~ Psalm 121:8

The heavens declare the glory of God;
the skies proclaim the work of His hands.

~ Psalm 19:1

The LORD is my light and my salvation – whom shall I fear?
The LORD is the stronghold of my life – of whom shall I be afraid?

~ Psalm 27:1

One thing I ask of the LORD, this is what I seek:
that I may dwell in the house of the LORD all the days of my life.

~ Psalm 27:4

Taste and see that the LORD is good;
blessed is the man who takes refuge in Him.

~ Psalm 34:8

God has made everything beautiful in its time.
~ Ecclesiastes 3:11

Praise be to the God and Father of our Lord Jesus Christ,
who has blessed us with every spiritual blessing in Christ.

~ Ephesians 1:3

My help comes from the LORD, the Maker of heaven and earth.

~Psalm 121:2

Be strong in the Lord and in His mighty power.

~ Ephesians 6:10

Rejoice in the Lord always. I will say it again: Rejoice!

~ Philippians 4:4

Faith is being sure of what we hope for and certain of what we do not see.

~ Hebrews 11:1

"Do not let your hearts be troubled. Trust in God; trust also in Me."
~ John 14:1

"Let your light shine before men, that they may see your good deeds and praise your Father in heaven."

~ Matthew 5:16

"Blessed are those who hunger and thirst for righteousness,
for they will be filled."

~ Matthew 5:6

"Seek first His kingdom and His righteousness,
and all these things will be given to you as well."

~ Matthew 6:33

"Ask and it will be given to you; seek and you will find;
knock and the door will be opened to you."

~ Matthew 7:7

From the fullness of His grace we have all received one blessing after another.

~ John 1:16

Shout for joy to the LORD, all the earth.

~ Psalm 100:1

Come, let us sing for joy to the LORD; let us shout aloud
to the Rock of our salvation.

~ Psalm 95:1

How many are Your works, O Lord! In wisdom You made them all;
the earth is full of Your creatures.

~ Psalm 104:24

The fear of the LORD is the beginning of wisdom;
all who follow His precepts have good understanding.

~ Psalm 111:10

You will keep in perfect peace him whose mind is steadfast,
because he trusts in You.

~ Isaiah 26:3

The LORD is my shepherd, I shall not be in want.

~ Psalm 23:1

In all things God works for the good of those who love Him,
who have been called according to His purpose.

~ Romans 8:28

The eternal God is your refuge, and underneath are the everlasting arms.

~ Deuteronomy 33:27

"Be strong and courageous. Do not be terrified; for the LORD
your God will be with you wherever you go."

~ Joshua 1:9

You have made known to me the path of life; You will fill me with
joy in Your presence, with eternal pleasures at Your right hand.

~ Psalm 16:11

As for God, His way is perfect; the word of the LORD is flawless.
He is a shield for all who take refuge in Him.

~ 2 Samuel 22:31

Ascribe to the LORD the glory due His name. Bring an offering
and come before Him; worship the LORD in the splendor of His holiness.

~ 1 Chronicles 16:29

Shout for joy to the LORD, burst into jubilant song with music.

~ Psalm 98:4

He will yet fill your mouth with laughter and your lips with shouts of joy.

~ Job 8:21

O Lord, our Lord, how majestic is Your name in all the earth!

~ Psalm 8:9

The LORD will watch over your coming and going both now and forevermore.

~ Psalm 121:8

The heavens declare the glory of God;
the skies proclaim the work of His hands.

~ Psalm 19:1

The LORD is my light and my salvation – whom shall I fear?
The LORD is the stronghold of my life – of whom shall I be afraid?

~ Psalm 27:1

One thing I ask of the LORD, this is what I seek:
that I may dwell in the house of the LORD all the days of my life.

~ Psalm 27:4

Taste and see that the LORD is good;
blessed is the man who takes refuge in Him.

~ Psalm 34:8

God has made everything beautiful in its time.

~ Ecclesiastes 3:11

Praise be to the God and Father of our Lord Jesus Christ,
who has blessed us with every spiritual blessing in Christ.

~ Ephesians 1:3

My help comes from the LORD, the Maker of heaven and earth.

~Psalm 121:2

Be strong in the Lord and in His mighty power.

~ Ephesians 6:10

Rejoice in the Lord always. I will say it again: Rejoice!

~ Philippians 4:4

Faith is being sure of what we hope for and certain of what we do not see.
~ Hebrews 11:1

"Do not let your hearts be troubled. Trust in God; trust also in Me."

~ John 14:1

"Let your light shine before men, that they may see
your good deeds and praise your Father in heaven."

~ Matthew 5:16

"Blessed are those who hunger and thirst for righteousness,
for they will be filled."

~ Matthew 5:6

"Seek first His kingdom and His righteousness,
and all these things will be given to you as well."
~ Matthew 6:33

"Ask and it will be given to you; seek and you will find;
knock and the door will be opened to you."

~ Matthew 7:7

From the fullness of His grace we have all received one blessing after another.

~ John 1:16

Shout for joy to the LORD, all the earth.

~ Psalm 100:1

Come, let us sing for joy to the LORD; let us shout aloud
to the Rock of our salvation.

~ Psalm 95:1

How many are Your works, O Lord! In wisdom You made them all;
the earth is full of Your creatures.

~ Psalm 104:24

The fear of the LORD is the beginning of wisdom;
all who follow His precepts have good understanding.

You will keep in perfect peace him whose mind is steadfast,
because he trusts in You.

~ Isaiah 26:3

The Lord is my shepherd, I shall not be in want.

~ Psalm 23:1

In all things God works for the good of those who love Him,
who have been called according to His purpose.

~ Romans 8:28

The eternal God is your refuge, and underneath are the everlasting arms.

~ Deuteronomy 33:27

"Be strong and courageous. Do not be terrified; for the LORD
your God will be with you wherever you go."

~ Joshua 1:9

You have made known to me the path of life; You will fill me with joy in Your presence, with eternal pleasures at Your right hand.

~ Psalm 16:11

As for God, His way is perfect; the word of the Lord is flawless.
He is a shield for all who take refuge in Him.

~ 2 Samuel 22:31

Ascribe to the Lord the glory due His name. Bring an offering
and come before Him; worship the Lord in the splendor of His holiness.

~ 1 Chronicles 16:29

Shout for joy to the LORD, burst into jubilant song with music.

~ Psalm 98:4

He will yet fill your mouth with laughter and your lips with shouts of joy.

~ Job 8:21

O Lord, our Lord, how majestic is Your name in all the earth!

~ Psalm 8:9

The LORD will watch over your coming and going both now and forevermore.
~ Psalm 121:8

The heavens declare the glory of God;
the skies proclaim the work of His hands.

~ Psalm 19:1

The LORD is my light and my salvation – whom shall I fear?
The LORD is the stronghold of my life – of whom shall I be afraid?

~ Psalm 27:1

One thing I ask of the LORD, this is what I seek:
that I may dwell in the house of the LORD all the days of my life.

~ Psalm 27:4

Taste and see that the LORD is good;
blessed is the man who takes refuge in Him.

~ Psalm 34:8

God has made everything beautiful in its time.

~ Ecclesiastes 3:11

Praise be to the God and Father of our Lord Jesus Christ,
who has blessed us with every spiritual blessing in Christ.

~ Ephesians 1:3

My help comes from the LORD, the Maker of heaven and earth.

~Psalm 121:2

Be strong in the Lord and in His mighty power.

~ Ephesians 6:10

Rejoice in the Lord always. I will say it again: Rejoice!

~ Philippians 4:4

Faith is being sure of what we hope for and certain of what we do not see.

~ Hebrews 11:1

"Do not let your hearts be troubled. Trust in God; trust also in Me."

~ John 14:1

"Let your light shine before men, that they may see your good deeds and praise your Father in heaven."

~ Matthew 5:16

"Blessed are those who hunger and thirst for righteousness,
for they will be filled."

~ Matthew 5:6

"Seek first His kingdom and His righteousness,
and all these things will be given to you as well."

~ Matthew 6:33

"Ask and it will be given to you; seek and you will find;
knock and the door will be opened to you."

~ Matthew 7:7

From the fullness of His grace we have all received one blessing after another.

~ John 1:16

Shout for joy to the LORD, all the earth.

~ Psalm 100:1

Come, let us sing for joy to the LORD; let us shout aloud
to the Rock of our salvation.

~ Psalm 95:1

How many are Your works, O Lord! In wisdom You made them all;
the earth is full of Your creatures.

~ Psalm 104:24

The fear of the LORD is the beginning of wisdom;
all who follow His precepts have good understanding.

~ Psalm 111:10

You will keep in perfect peace him whose mind is steadfast,
because he trusts in You.

~ Isaiah 26:3

The Lord is my shepherd, I shall not be in want.

~ Psalm 23:1

In all things God works for the good of those who love Him,
who have been called according to His purpose.

~ Romans 8:28

The eternal God is your refuge, and underneath are the everlasting arms.

~ Deuteronomy 33:27

"Be strong and courageous. Do not be terrified; for the Lord
your God will be with you wherever you go."

~ Joshua 1:9

You have made known to me the path of life; You will fill me with
joy in Your presence, with eternal pleasures at Your right hand.

~ Psalm 16:11

As for God, His way is perfect; the word of the LORD is flawless.
He is a shield for all who take refuge in Him.

~ 2 Samuel 22:31

Ascribe to the LORD the glory due His name. Bring an offering
and come before Him; worship the LORD in the splendor of His holiness.

~ 1 Chronicles 16:29

Shout for joy to the LORD, burst into jubilant song with music.

~ Psalm 98:4

He will yet fill your mouth with laughter and your lips with shouts of joy.

~ Job 8:21

O Lord, our Lord, how majestic is Your name in all the earth!

~ Psalm 8:9

The LORD will watch over your coming and going both now and forevermore.

~ Psalm 121:8

The heavens declare the glory of God;
the skies proclaim the work of His hands.

~ Psalm 19:1

The Lord is my light and my salvation – whom shall I fear?
The Lord is the stronghold of my life – of whom shall I be afraid?

~ Psalm 27:1

One thing I ask of the Lord, this is what I seek:
that I may dwell in the house of the Lord all the days of my life.

~ Psalm 27:4

Taste and see that the LORD is good;
blessed is the man who takes refuge in Him.

~ Psalm 34:8

God has made everything beautiful in its time.

~ Ecclesiastes 3:11

Praise be to the God and Father of our Lord Jesus Christ,
who has blessed us with every spiritual blessing in Christ.

~ Ephesians 1:3

My help comes from the LORD, the Maker of heaven and earth.

~Psalm 121:2

Be strong in the Lord and in His mighty power.

~ Ephesians 6:10

Rejoice in the Lord always. I will say it again: Rejoice!

~ Philippians 4:4

Faith is being sure of what we hope for and certain of what we do not see.
~ Hebrews 11:1

"Do not let your hearts be troubled. Trust in God; trust also in Me."

~ John 14:1

"Let your light shine before men, that they may see your good deeds and praise your Father in heaven."

~ Matthew 5:16

"Blessed are those who hunger and thirst for righteousness,
for they will be filled."

~ Matthew 5:6

"Seek first His kingdom and His righteousness,
and all these things will be given to you as well."

~ Matthew 6:33

"Ask and it will be given to you; seek and you will find;
knock and the door will be opened to you."

~ Matthew 7:7

From the fullness of His grace we have all received one blessing after another.

~ John 1:16

Shout for joy to the Lord, all the earth.

~ Psalm 100:1

Come, let us sing for joy to the LORD; let us shout aloud
to the Rock of our salvation.

~ Psalm 95:1

How many are Your works, O Lord! In wisdom You made them all;
the earth is full of Your creatures.

~ Psalm 104:24

The fear of the LORD is the beginning of wisdom;
all who follow His precepts have good understanding.

~ Psalm 111:10

You will keep in perfect peace him whose mind is steadfast,
because he trusts in You.

~ Isaiah 26:3

The Lord is my shepherd, I shall not be in want.

~ Psalm 23:1

In all things God works for the good of those who love Him,
who have been called according to His purpose.

~ Romans 8:28

The eternal God is your refuge, and underneath are the everlasting arms.

~ Deuteronomy 33:27

"Be strong and courageous. Do not be terrified; for the LORD
your God will be with you wherever you go."

~ Joshua 1:9

You have made known to me the path of life; You will fill me with joy in Your presence, with eternal pleasures at Your right hand.

~ Psalm 16:11

As for God, His way is perfect; the word of the LORD is flawless.
He is a shield for all who take refuge in Him.

~ 2 Samuel 22:31

Ascribe to the LORD the glory due His name. Bring an offering
and come before Him; worship the LORD in the splendor of His holiness.

~ 1 Chronicles 16:29

Shout for joy to the LORD, burst into jubilant song with music.

~ Psalm 98:4

He will yet fill your mouth with laughter and your lips with shouts of joy.

~ Job 8:21

O LORD, our Lord, how majestic is Your name in all the earth!

~ Psalm 8:9

The LORD will watch over your coming and going both now and forevermore.

~ Psalm 121:8

The heavens declare the glory of God;
the skies proclaim the work of His hands.

~ Psalm 19:1

The LORD is my light and my salvation – whom shall I fear?
The LORD is the stronghold of my life – of whom shall I be afraid?

~ Psalm 27:1

One thing I ask of the LORD, this is what I seek:
that I may dwell in the house of the LORD all the days of my life.

~ Psalm 27:4

Taste and see that the LORD is good;
blessed is the man who takes refuge in Him.

~ Psalm 34:8

God has made everything beautiful in its time.

~ Ecclesiastes 3:11

Praise be to the God and Father of our Lord Jesus Christ,
who has blessed us with every spiritual blessing in Christ.

~ Ephesians 1:3

My help comes from the LORD, the Maker of heaven and earth.

~Psalm 121:2

Be strong in the Lord and in His mighty power.

~ Ephesians 6:10

Rejoice in the Lord always. I will say it again: Rejoice!

~ Philippians 4:4

Faith is being sure of what we hope for and certain of what we do not see.

~ Hebrews 11:1

"Do not let your hearts be troubled. Trust in God; trust also in Me."

~ John 14:1

"Let your light shine before men, that they may see your good deeds and praise your Father in heaven."

~ Matthew 5:16

"Blessed are those who hunger and thirst for righteousness,
for they will be filled."

~ Matthew 5:6

"Seek first His kingdom and His righteousness,
and all these things will be given to you as well."

~ Matthew 6:33

"Ask and it will be given to you; seek and you will find;
knock and the door will be opened to you."

~ Matthew 7:7

From the fullness of His grace we have all received one blessing after another.

~ John 1:16

Shout for joy to the LORD, all the earth.

~ Psalm 100:1

Come, let us sing for joy to the LORD; let us shout aloud
to the Rock of our salvation.

~ Psalm 95:1

How many are Your works, O Lord! In wisdom You made them all;
the earth is full of Your creatures.

~ Psalm 104:24

The fear of the Lord is the beginning of wisdom;
all who follow His precepts have good understanding.

~ Psalm 111:10

You will keep in perfect peace him whose mind is steadfast,
because he trusts in You.

~ Isaiah 26:3

The Lord is my shepherd, I shall not be in want.

~ Psalm 23:1

In all things God works for the good of those who love Him,
who have been called according to His purpose.

~ Romans 8:28

The eternal God is your refuge, and underneath are the everlasting arms.

~ Deuteronomy 33:27

_____

_____

_____

_____

_____

_____

_____

_____

_____

_____

_____

_____

_____

_____

_____

_____

_____

_____

_____

_____

_____

_____

"Be strong and courageous. Do not be terrified; for the LORD
your God will be with you wherever you go."

~ Joshua 1:9

You have made known to me the path of life; You will fill me with
joy in Your presence, with eternal pleasures at Your right hand.

~ Psalm 16:11

As for God, His way is perfect; the word of the LORD is flawless.
He is a shield for all who take refuge in Him.

~ 2 Samuel 22:31

Ascribe to the LORD the glory due His name. Bring an offering
and come before Him; worship the LORD in the splendor of His holiness.

~ 1 Chronicles 16:29

Shout for joy to the LORD, burst into jubilant song with music.

~ Psalm 98:4

He will yet fill your mouth with laughter and your lips with shouts of joy.

~ Job 8:21

O Lord, our Lord, how majestic is Your name in all the earth!

~ Psalm 8:9

The LORD will watch over your coming and going both now and forevermore.

~ Psalm 121:8

The heavens declare the glory of God;
the skies proclaim the work of His hands.

~ Psalm 19:1

The LORD is my light and my salvation – whom shall I fear?
The LORD is the stronghold of my life – of whom shall I be afraid?

~ Psalm 27:1

One thing I ask of the LORD, this is what I seek:
that I may dwell in the house of the LORD all the days of my life.

~ Psalm 27:4

Taste and see that the LORD is good;
blessed is the man who takes refuge in Him.

~ Psalm 34:8

God has made everything beautiful in its time.

~ Ecclesiastes 3:11

Praise be to the God and Father of our Lord Jesus Christ,
who has blessed us with every spiritual blessing in Christ.

~ Ephesians 1:3

My help comes from the LORD, the Maker of heaven and earth.

~Psalm 121:2

Be strong in the Lord and in His mighty power.

~ Ephesians 6:10

Rejoice in the Lord always. I will say it again: Rejoice!

~ Philippians 4:4

Faith is being sure of what we hope for and certain of what we do not see.

~ Hebrews 11:1

"Do not let your hearts be troubled. Trust in God; trust also in Me."

~ John 14:1

"Let your light shine before men, that they may see
your good deeds and praise your Father in heaven."
~ Matthew 5:16

"Blessed are those who hunger and thirst for righteousness,
for they will be filled."

~ Matthew 5:6

"Seek first His kingdom and His righteousness,
and all these things will be given to you as well."

~ Matthew 6:33

"Ask and it will be given to you; seek and you will find;
knock and the door will be opened to you."

~ Matthew 7:7

From the fullness of His grace we have all received one blessing after another.
~ John 1:16

Shout for joy to the LORD, all the earth.

~ Psalm 100:1

Come, let us sing for joy to the LORD; let us shout aloud
to the Rock of our salvation.

~ Psalm 95:1

How many are Your works, O LORD! In wisdom You made them all;
the earth is full of Your creatures.

~ Psalm 104:24

The fear of the Lord is the beginning of wisdom;
all who follow His precepts have good understanding.

~ Psalm 111:10

You will keep in perfect peace him whose mind is steadfast,
because he trusts in You.

~ Isaiah 26:3